Editor's Note

Dear Readers,

As we embark on the next chapter of our magazine, I wanted to take a moment to reflect on the importance of transformation and growth. In these pages, you'll find a wealth of insights and inspiration to help you on your own journey towards personal and professional transformation.

We believe that each one of us has the power to change and grow, not only as individuals but also as a global community. Whether it's embracing a healthier lifestyle, cultivating positive relationships, or exploring new hobbies, our aim is to provide you with the tools and guidance to thrive in every aspect of your life.

Personal growth and self-discovery are at the heart of our mission. We understand that navigating through life's challenges requires resilience, adaptability, and the willingness to embrace change. Through thought-provoking articles, expert advice, and real-life stories, we hope to inspire and empower you to reach your fullest potential.

But it doesn't stop there! We also recognize the importance of professional growth in today's ever-evolving world. With insights from industry leaders, innovative ideas, and practical tips, we aim to equip you with the knowledge and skills needed to flourish in your career.

As you peruse the pages of this magazine, I encourage you to take a moment to reflect on your own personal journey. Embrace the exciting transformations that lie ahead and consider the

myriad of possibilities waiting for you. Remember, transformation is a continuous process, and every step forward is an opportunity for growth and self-improvement.

We would love to hear your stories of transformation and how the magazine has inspired positive change in your life.

Please share your experiences with us at editor@vmhmagazine.com

Thank you for being a part of VMH Magazine's journey, and here's to a future filled with endless possibilities!

Vikki Jones

Editor-in-Chief

CONTENTS

Photo Credit: Vikki Jones

EXCLUSIVE

ELEVATION STRATEGIES

TAKE YOUR BUSINESS
TO NEW HEIGHTS

VIKKIMJONES.COM

PROSTATE CANCER: KNOW THE WARNING SIGNS, WHEN TO GET SCREENED

American Cancer Society

Prostate cancer is the second leading cause of cancer death among men in the United States. According to the latest research from scientists at the American Cancer Society (ACS), more than 288,000 men will be diagnosed with the disease this year, with close to 35,000 deaths. Black men are two times more likely to die from the disease than White men and have the highest death rate for prostate cancer of any racial and ethnic group.

Prostate cancer is the second leading cause of cancer death among men in the United States. According to the latest research from scientists at the <u>American Cancer Society</u> (ACS), more than 288,000 men will be diagnosed with the disease this year, with close to 35,000 deaths. Black men are two times more likely to die from the disease than White men and have the highest death rate for prostate cancer of any racial and ethnic group. However, when prostate cancer is detected early, the odds of survival are high. In fact, more than 3.5 million men diagnosed with the disease in the U.S. are still alive today.

Renowned prostate cancer researcher Dr. Lorelei Mucci is the director of strategic research partnerships at the American Cancer Society. Her role includes leading an ACS initiative called <u>IMPACT</u>, or "Improving Mortality Toward Prostate Cancer Together" to address the alarming negative trends in prostate cancer incidence and disparities. For Prostate Cancer Awareness Month Dr. Mucci reviews the signs and symptoms of prostate cancer, including important information about risk factors, PSA screening, and more:

1-Why is it important every September during Prostate Cancer Awarenesss Month to help people learn about the disease?

Despite the alarming statistics concerning the disease, there are opportunities for prevention, early detection, and treatment to improve survival and survivorship and to reduce the burden this cancer has across the U.S. and the globe. Prostate Cancer Awareness Month is so important to have a focused time for men and their families to share knowledge, experiences, and state of science on this important cancer. It is also a time to reflect upon the people who have been impacted by prostate cancer and who have lost their lives to the disease. Also, Prostate Cancer Awareness Month can be an important stimulus to remind public health professionals and government leaders of the need to invest in prevention, early detection, treatment, and improving survivorship.

2- What are the warning signs of prostate cancer?

For some men, prostate cancer may lead to urinary problems, such as having difficulty starting urination or urinating frequently, or pain during ejaculation. This is because of the location of the prostate close to the bladder and urethra. These symptoms and signs also occur with non-cancer conditions, so it is important to follow up with a physician to find out what might be causing these symptoms. If a cancer has already grown beyond the prostate, there may be pain in the hips, back, or other areas that does not go away. For most people, however, there are no signs or symptoms indicating prostate cancer and the cancer is diagnosed with a biopsy following an abnormal blood test.

3- Who is at risk for prostate cancer?

Anyone with a prostate is at risk of prostate cancer, and it is one of the most common cancers. There are some groups that are at higher risk of prostate cancer. For example, our latest research shows Black men and those of African ancestry are 70% more likely to be diagnosed with prostate cancer. Also, the risk of prostate cancer gets higher with age. In addition, people with a family history of prostate cancer (such as in their brother or father) as well as a family history of breast cancer in a sister or mother, are at higher risk of prostate cancer. Part of the family history is due to inherited genetic factors or gene mutations that we now know about. An important note is that while age, family history, and race/ancestry are not modifiable factors (things you can change), there are other factors such as maintaining a healthy body weight, not smoking, and being physically active that can help to offset this higher risk.

4- What is the treatment for prostate cancer? Have there been any advancements in treating the disease?

There are effective treatments for prostate cancer. When the cancer is still confined to the prostate (localized), surgery (radical prostatectomy) and certain forms of radiation are useful to treat and cure prostate cancer. For men who have a low risk of their prostate cancer metastasizing, active surveillance - in which a patient is closely monitored for signs of cancer progression - can also be an important treatment to consider. When the cancer is more aggressive, there are additional therapies that are used, including therapies that target hormonal pathways, chemotherapy, immunotherapy, and radiopharmaceutical therapies. In fact, this is an exciting time in prostate cancer with substantial progress in the discovery and approval of new therapies over the past 5-10 years, as well as several other therapies being developed.

5- Is there a screening test for prostate cancer? Why is it important to catch it early?

Currently, the main screening test for prostate cancer involves taking a blood sample and testing it for the level of a marker called prostate-specific antigen (PSA). Higher levels of PSA in the blood can indicate prostate cancer, but also may be higher in benign conditions such as an enlarged prostate, so it is important to follow up with a doctor to discuss the results and the next steps.

There is good evidence showing that regular PSA screening can reduce prostate cancer mortality, including from randomized trials. However, there is some controversy with screening for prostate cancer since the test can pick up slower-growing cancers that will never lead to harm. An area of active research now is aiming to do more effective screening approaches, targeting the men who are at the highest risk of prostate cancer and then also safely letting people know they can screen less regularly. The ACS launched the "I Love You, Get Screened" campaign to encourage everyone to talk to their loved ones about cancer screening.

6- What age should men be screened for prostate cancer?

The ACS recommends that men at average risk for prostate cancer discuss the benefits and limitations of screening with their healthcare provider at age 50. Men at high risk (which includes Black men in general and any man with a first-degree relative who had prostate cancer before age 65) should have the conversation at age 45. Black men with a family history of breast, ovarian, or prostate cancer, and men with more than one first-degree relative who had prostate cancer at an early age should discuss screening at age 40. Detecting prostate cancer early can lead to more effective treatment and improved outcomes. *For more information on prostate cancer, go to www.cancer.org/cancer/types/prostate-cancer.html.*

SIMPLIFY YOUR HOLIDAY HOSTING FROM START TO FINISH

Hosting a major holiday event is no small effort. It requires close attention to detail from planning, cooking and cleaning to entertaining guests on the big day. Fortunately, just like any good recipe, approaching your hosting duties one step at a time can allow you to create a magnificent final product.

This Thanksgiving, the experts at Finish are helping hosts everywhere get organized, from the initial planning all the way through clean up, with the Ultimate Thanksgiving Timer. Created in partnership with Gaby Dalkin of "What's Gaby Cooking," it's a personalized hosting timeline designed to help hosts stay on track up to and throughout the big day.

"I've been hosting holiday gatherings for years and know from firsthand experience that even capable hosts struggle to time everything just right," Dalkin said. "From planning your menu and designing your tablescape to accommodating dietary restrictions and even serving dessert, the Ultimate Thanksgiving Timer will support hosts every step of the way this year."

Plan Your Guest List and Menu

Deciding how many guests you'll be serving and what you plan to serve are two essential details that will guide the rest of your planning. When creating your guest list, be realistic about how many are likely to attend and plan your menu for a few extra people so you don't run out of food. Your menu may also be influenced by how many guests you plan to host; a whole turkey is practical for a large group, but a turkey breast may be adequate for a more intimate gathering. Remember to send your invites at least three weeks ahead of the event so guests have plenty of time to respond and you can prepare your menu.

Start Grocery Shopping Early

The rush at the grocery store can be one of the most stressful parts of getting ready to host. Give yourself enough lead time by picking up pantry staples and beverages 1-2 weeks out so your kitchen is stocked for the big day. For perishables, get to the grocery store early in the day 1-2 days before hosting to beat the rush and avoid any last-minute grocery runs the morning of your gathering.

Maximize Prep Time

While it's likely the majority of your work will come on the big day, you can work ahead to reduce some of the load. For example, you can wash and chop vegetables for stuffing and other side dishes and store them overnight to minimize prep time in the morning. You can also use the quiet of the night before to tackle tasks like setting the table and organizing your seating chart, restocking towels and replenishing other essentials in the guest bathroom.

Enlist Help with Cooking

The day of your event is the perfect time to pull extra hands into the kitchen. A simple but tasty recipe like this Ultimate Cheesy Herb Sourdough Stuffing from Dalkin is a sure crowd-pleaser to add to your table this year. Once you establish your cooking space and find your rhythm, you may even find sharing the preparations with a loved one is a great way to bond and create special memories.

Make Cleanup a Cinch

A few simple tricks can help you maintain a relatively clean workspace and keep up with all the dishes you need to prepare a lavish meal. First, be sure to clean up as you go. It may be tempting to throw all of your dirty utensils and empty mixing bowls in a pile in the sink to deal with later, but taking a few minutes to scrape dishes and load the dishwasher as you go can help prevent a messy mountain from forming. That also means you'll be more likely to find a clean measuring cup or spoon when you move on to prepare the next dish.

Hosts have enough to worry about, so let your dishwasher do the hard work and pull in reinforcements to help clean up while you relax after a long day. Use a detergent that works in the toughest conditions, from burnt-on stains to old dishwashers and hard water, like Finish Ultimate. It's the only dish detergent tab with CycleSync technology that releases the right ingredient at the right time to work with your dishwasher.

You can skip the rinse, even on tough stains like cranberry sauce and gravy, and save up to 20 gallons of water. Hosts are invited to put Finish Ultimate to the test and take the Ultimate Thanksgiving Challenge; if it can't tackle your burnt-on stains, the meal is on Finish via a rebate of up to $30.

For more hosting tips and tricks, visit UltimateThanksgivingExperience.com.

Ultimate Cheesy Herb Sourdough Stuffing

Recipe courtesy of "What's Gaby Cooking" on behalf of Finish

- 1 loaf sourdough bread with crust, cut into 1-inch cubes (roughly 8 cups)
- 10 tablespoons butter
- 2 shallots, finely sliced
- 2 celery stalks, finely chopped
- 2 bunches green onions, thinly sliced
- 3/4 cup chopped fresh Italian parsley
- 2 tablespoons chopped fresh oregano
- 2 tablespoons chopped fresh sage
- 2 tablespoons chopped fresh thyme
- 3 large garlic cloves, minced
- 2 teaspoons coarse kosher salt
- 1 teaspoon freshly ground black pepper
- 3 large eggs
- 2 cups chicken broth, divided
- 6 ounces coarsely grated Parmesan cheese

Preheat oven to 375 F. On large, rimmed baking sheet, spread ripped or cubed bread. Bake until bread is dry, about 15 minutes. Cool. Leave oven on.

In heavy skillet over medium heat, melt butter. Add shallots and celery; saute 5-6 minutes. Add green onions, parsley, oregano, sage, thyme, garlic, salt and pepper; saute until celery is tender, 6-8 minutes.

Generously grease large skillet or ceramic baking dish. Place bread cubes in large bowl. Add warm vegetable mixture; toss to combine.

In medium bowl, whisk eggs and 3/4 cup broth. Add egg mixture to stuffing and toss to coat. Mix in Parmesan.

Add 1/2-3/4 cup broth to stuffing if dry. Transfer to skillet or ceramic baking dish. Cover with buttered foil. Bake 30 minutes. Remove foil; bake until golden, about 30 minutes. Serve in baking vessel or transfer to serving platter.

PlayersTV, the premier destination for athlete-driven content, has taken a monumental stride in fan engagement with its groundbreaking Fan Ownership Initiative. This initiative marks a historic moment in sports history, as PlayersTV becomes the world's first athlete fan-owned media company network.

The impressive roster of investor-athletes at PlayersTV reads like a who's who of sports legends. With over 50 NFL, NBA, WNBA, and MLB athletes on board, including Kyrie Irving, Chris Paul, Dwyane Wade, Damian Lillard, Travis Kelce, Vernon Davis, Deandre Jordan, Carmelo Anthony, Natasha Cloud, Angel McCoughtry, AJ Andrews, and many more, PlayersTV has garnered the support of some of the biggest names in the sports world.

These athlete investors not only recognize the significance of this initiative but also endorse its potential to revolutionize the media landscape. Their involvement speaks volumes about the trust and belief they have in PlayersTV's mission to bring athletes and fans closer together.

Deron Guidrey, the visionary founder of PlayersTV, expressed his excitement about the initiative, stating, "Today marks an exciting milestone as we open the doors for fans to become proud owners in PlayersTV, our very own athlete-owned media company. This journey has always been about bringing athletes and fans closer together, and now, by becoming owners, our fans are not just spectators, but integral players in shaping the future and redefining athlete media."

Co-founder Collin Castellaw echoed Guidrey's sentiments, emphasizing that this initiative goes beyond business. "This is more than a business move; it's a movement that celebrates the unity of athletes and fans. We're breaking down barriers and creating an ecosystem where everyone's passion is reflected in every aspect of PlayersTV."

With the Fan Ownership Initiative, PlayersTV is set to redefine the future of sports media. By empowering fans to become shareholders and owners, the network is transforming them from passive viewers into active participants and stakeholders. This move not only strengthens the bond between sports stars and their unwavering supporters but also amplifies the voices of fans and allows them to play a role in shaping the network's future endeavors.

Furthermore, this initiative opens up new avenues for fan engagement and interaction. As stakeholders, fans have the opportunity to provide feedback, suggestions, and ideas for new shows and programming, ensuring that the content reflects their preferences and interests.

PlayersTV's Fan Ownership Initiative is a game-changer in the sports media industry. With the support of an impressive roster of athlete investors, PlayersTV is creating a stronger, more inclusive community and reshaping the future of sports media. This historic move sets a precedent for other networks and demonstrates PlayersTV's commitment to innovation and fan engagement. As the first athlete fan-owned media company, *For more information, visit: www.playerstv.com/invest*.

SHE CREATED HER LANE

Vikki Jones, a tenacious and resourceful individual, has defied all odds to create a successful multimedia and publishing world using minimal resources. Armed with nothing but a flip phone, a donated laptop, and free Wi-Fi at the public library, she has showcased that with a clear vision, eliminating distractions, and regularly reevaluating her life, surroundings, and relationships, one can elevate themselves to great heights.

Throughout her inspiring journey, Vikki has taken numerous actionable steps, such as attending elite conferences both domestically and internationally to learn from global speakers like Sir Richard Branson, Former President Barack Obama, and Jensen Huang, Founder of NVIDIA. Additionally, she has been fortunate enough to conduct interviews with luminaries like Harris Rosen of Rosen Hotels. By intentionally seeking out the best opportunities to learn and meticulously managing her finances, Vikki built her company while expanding her knowledge and skills.

Nevertheless, Vikki's remarkable achievements and personal growth all stem from the uniqueness of her heart, fueled by an unwavering passion and

talent that she had always known resided within it. Continuously challenging herself, refining her creative skills, and devoting time to self-discovery have been integral to her ascension. "Waiting for external factors, such as funding or investors, to propel me forward was never an option. I have only one life, and I must utilize my wit to navigate the path that leads to my desired destination. Otherwise, I would never attain what I truly deserve," Vikki asserts.

Vikki's self-discovery journey has unveiled countless revelations that have transformed her into an invaluable contributor to society. Her unyielding love for technology and her innate ability to harness its power for personal gain has been instrumental in her growth. Allowing herself ample time to learn, make mistakes, and identify more effective strategies has been a consistent theme throughout her rise.

"I find joy in continually learning about the incredible opportunities that life and the business world have to offer, especially from diverse corners of the globe. Relocating my company to more advantageous geographical locations has also served as a catalyst for my personal and professional development," Vikki shares.

One of Vikki's most impactful decisions was to distance herself from influences that could hinder her individual growth. Moving away from the opinions and expectations of others allowed her the space and solitude necessary for introspection and self-guidance. "I needed to ensure that I remained aligned with myself, constantly discovering and uncovering layers of my being. This practice has always served as my guiding light, informing my actions and charting my path forward. It is not always about the allure of money or the tasks at hand. Sometimes, prioritizing self-awareness and self-growth takes precedence over all tangible aspects," Vikki passionately explains.

Vikki's inspiring journey has not only taught her invaluable lessons but also illuminated the importance of perseverance, resilience, and staying true to oneself. Throughout her quest for success, she has shown that resourcefulness goes beyond material possessions. It encompasses a boundless determination, an insatiable appetite for knowledge, and an unwavering belief in one's abilities.

Vikki Jones is an exceptional individual who has carved her own path with little resources but abundant determination and passion. By embracing her uniqueness, constantly challenging herself, and prioritizing self-discovery, she has defied expectations and built a thriving multimedia and publishing empire. Her inspiring story reminds us that success is not limited by our circumstances, but rather by the powerful combination of perseverance, resourcefulness, and an unwavering belief in one's abilities. As we navigate our own journeys, let us draw inspiration from Vikki's incredible example and strive to create our own lanes with courage and determination. Learn more about Vikki Jones at: vikkimjones.com

Takeaways:

- Clear Vision: Maintaining a clear and unwavering vision for your life and aspirations is crucial in navigating the noise and distractions that can hinder progress.
- Self-Discovery: Dedicate time and effort to learn more about yourself. Understanding your strengths, passions, and areas for growth will help you make informed decisions and shape your path to success.
- Continuous Learning: Embrace a mindset of lifelong learning. Seek out opportunities to expand your knowledge, gain diverse perspectives, and stay at the forefront of your industry.
- Resourcefulness: Remember that success is not limited by the resources you possess, but by your determination, resilience, and ability to make the most out of what you have.
- Prioritize Alignment: Stay true to yourself and your dreams, even if it means distancing yourself from the expectations and opinions of others. Aligning your choices with your core values will help you make meaningful progress.

Jay Shetty

REMINDS US THAT TRUE SUCCESS LIES IN GOING BEYOND TRANSACTIONS AND EMBRACING A HIGHER PURPOSE.

It's easy to get caught up in the pursuit of immediate results and quick sales. However, research and wisdom from thought leaders like Jay Shetty remind us that true success lies in going beyond transactions and embracing a higher purpose.

According to Shetty, purpose is not just about what you do; it's about the profound transformation you create and the impact you have on people's lives. When individuals and companies prioritize purpose, something magical happens. Employees are more likely to be drawn to them, trust them, and stay loyal.

Studies have shown that companies that prioritize purpose tend to have higher employee engagement and satisfaction levels. When employees feel a sense of purpose in their work, they are more motivated, productive, and fulfilled. They are not just driven by financial rewards but by the knowledge that they are making a meaningful difference in the world.

Furthermore, purpose-driven companies often attract customers who resonate with their values and mission. Consumers today are becoming increasingly conscious of the impact their choices have on society and the environment. They seek out brands and businesses that align with their values and are committed to making a positive difference. So, how can individuals and businesses avoid falling into the transactional trap and embrace purpose?

First, it's essential to define your purpose beyond financial gains. Ask yourself: What impact do I want to have on people's lives? How can I make a difference in the world? By shifting your focus from transactions to transformation, you can uncover a deeper sense of meaning and fulfillment in your work.

Second, communicate your purpose to your employees, customers, and stakeholders. Be transparent about your values and the positive change you aim to create. This transparency builds trust and fosters a sense of connection with those who share your purpose.

Next, integrate purpose into every aspect of your business. From product development to customer service, let purpose guide your decisions and actions. Align your strategies with your mission, and ensure that every interaction reflects your commitment to making a difference.

Lastly, measure and celebrate the impact you are making.

TAKEAWAYS:

According to Jay Shetty, purpose goes beyond "what you do; it's about the massive transformation you create and the impact you have on people's lives."

Research shows that when companies prioritize purpose, magic happens! Employees are more likely to want to work for them, trust them, and stay loyal.

Don't fall into the transactional trap! Your purpose should be about making a difference, not just a quick sale.

Regular assess how your purpose is translating into tangible results and positive change. Share these achievements with your team and stakeholders, reinforcing the sense of purpose and motivation.

In conclusion, purpose is not just a buzzword; it's a powerful force that can transform individuals and organizations. By embracing purpose beyond transactions, you can create a meaningful impact on people's lives, build trust, and foster loyalty. So, let go of the transactional trap and make a difference that lasts.

UNLOCK YOUR LITERARY POTENTIAL WITH
VMH PUBLISHING

At VMH Publishing, we stand as a beacon of intellectual excellence, fueling the literary world with our unwavering commitment to literary brilliance. As a distinguished publishing house, we are dedicated to unearthing the limitless potential of language and ushering in a new era of profound literary works.

Whether you're a reader seeking an enthralling narrative, an aspiring author yearning to be discovered, or a literary enthusiast eager to explore new horizons, VMH Publishing invites you to embark on a journey of literary discovery. Immerse yourself in thought-provoking stories, poetic prose, and insightful non-fiction that will leave an indelible mark on your mind and heart.

Visit our website, www.vmhpublishing.net, to explore our captivating catalog and join us in our mission to celebrate the power of words. Together, let's redefine literary excellence and shape the future of literature.

GH200 is the next version of the Grace Hopper superchip, which is designed to share the work of AI programs via a tight coupling of CPU and GPU.

"Everyone becomes a programmer; everyone becomes a creator."

The Future is Here: NVIDIA's Powerful AI Supercomputer and What it Means for Consumers

In a recent announcement, NVIDIA unveiled its amazing new AI supercomputer called the NVIDIA DGX GH200. This supercomputer has the ability to train the next generation of AI models and push the boundaries of technology. Jensen Huang, the CEO of NVIDIA, explains, "With the DGX GH200 AI supercomputer, we are expanding the frontier of AI and enabling digital engines that drive the modern economy."

So, what does this mean for consumers like you and me? Here's what you need to know:

1. Incredible Power: The NVIDIA DGX GH200 is incredibly powerful, capable of performing 1 exaflop of calculations. To put that in perspective, it can process information at a mind-bogglingly fast speed. This power enables researchers and scientists to tackle complex problems and make important breakthroughs.

2. Better AI Models: Thanks to its advanced technology, the DGX GH200 allows for the creation and training of larger AI models. This means that AI systems will become even smarter and more capable. For example, language translation and recommendation systems will improve, making our digital experiences more

personalized and efficient.

3. Transforming Industries: The DGX GH200 has the potential to revolutionize various industries such as healthcare, finance, transportation, and entertainment. It opens up new avenues for innovation, enabling organizations to use AI in ways we never thought possible. Imagine better medical diagnoses, more accurate financial predictions, and immersive virtual reality experiences.

4. Efficient Data Processing: The supercomputer's large memory capacity lets it process huge amounts of data quickly and efficiently. This means faster analysis and decision-making based on accurate information. For consumers, it could mean quicker response times from customer service bots or better personalized recommendations when shopping online.

Now, some people worry about the impact of AI on jobs. However, Jensen Huang reassures us, "Everyone becomes a programmer; everyone becomes a creator." What he means is that as AI evolves, it

opens up new opportunities for people to learn and adapt. While some jobs may be automated, new roles will emerge that require human creativity and expertise. NVIDIA's DGX GH200 represents a significant step forward in AI technology. It not only pushes the boundaries of what's possible but also presents exciting possibilities for consumers. This supercomputer has the potential to transform industries, improve AI models, and process data more efficiently. While concerns about job displacement exist, it's essential to recognize that AI also brings opportunities for innovation and learning. As we move into the future, the potential for everyone to become a programmer and creator becomes more attainable.

The future is here with NVIDIA's powerful AI supercomputer. With its immense capabilities and advancements, it has the potential to reshape the way we live, work, and interact with technology. So get ready for a future where AI becomes even more intelligent and where you might just find yourself becoming a programmer and creating amazing things.

Photo Credit: Vikki Jones

What is
THE SIMPLICITY OF INDULGING ONES PASSION

Ignite Passion for Your Work and Thrive

Passion Stimulates Value & Success If you have dreams, goals, and aspirational things you want to do with your life, go for it! Associate with people who will add to you and your goals versus take away from them. Get away from those folks that don't support your idea, and surround yourself with people that support and value you - help you grow.

@vmhmagazine

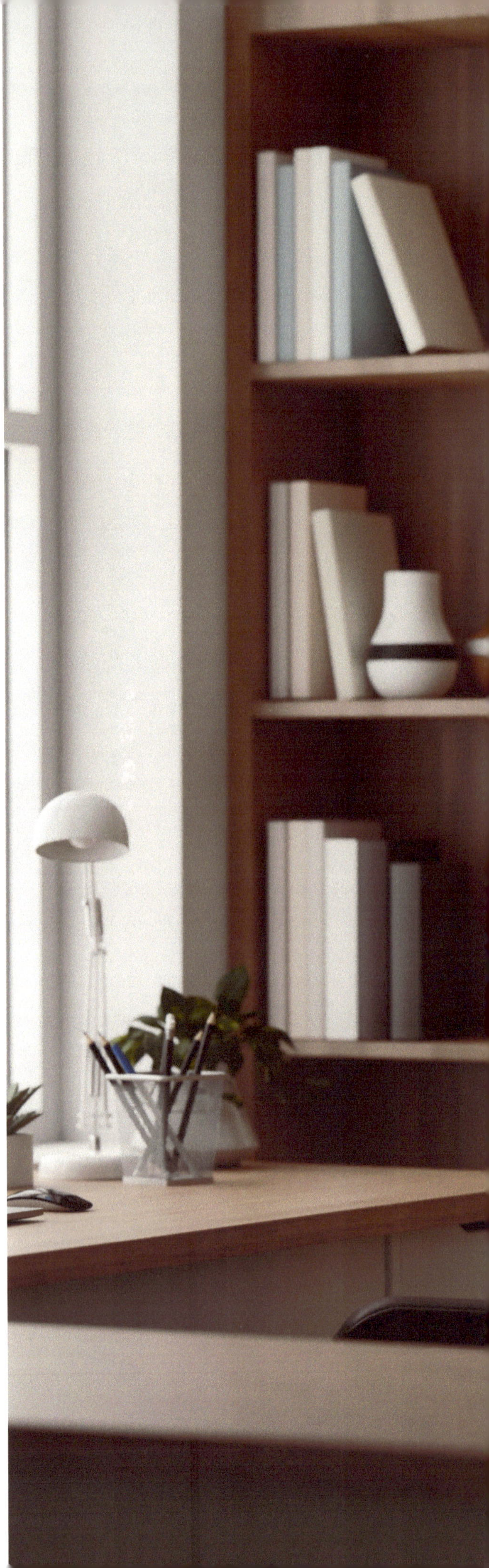

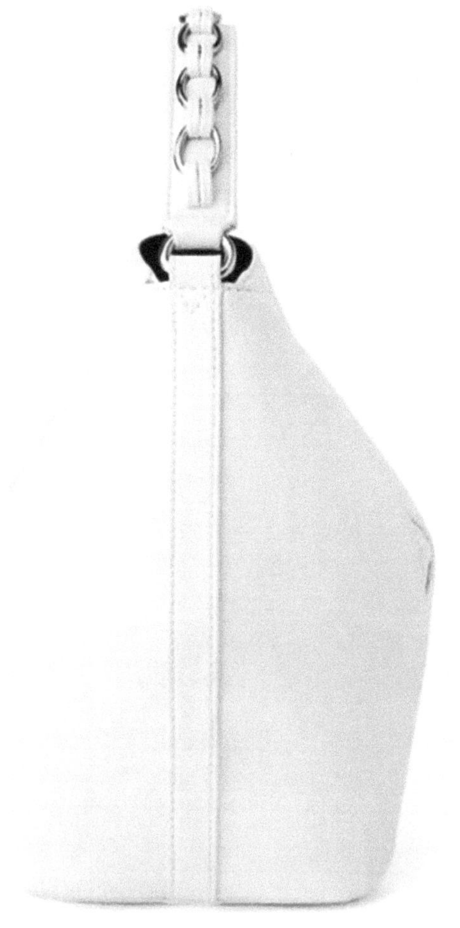

ELEGANT AND SOPHISTICATED

Introducing the White Vegan Leather Bucket Bag, an elegant and sophisticated accessory. Crafted with the finest vegan leather, this bag combines fashion with function, making it a must-have addition to your collection.

Features:

- **Ready for iPads, Tablets, and Important Items**: This bucket bag is thoughtfully designed to fit iPads, tablets, and any essential items you need by your side.
- **Additional Bit of Sophistication:** Exuding timeless elegance, this bag features a chain deco and faux leather handles, adding an extra touch of sophistication to your ensemble.
- **Spacious and Practical**: With dimensions of 10.5 inches in length, 6 inches in width, and 12 inches in height, this bag offers ample space for your belongings while maintaining a compact and fashionable appearance.
- **Magnetic Closures**: The bag is equipped with convenient magnetic closures, ensuring quick and secure access to your valuables while keeping them protected.

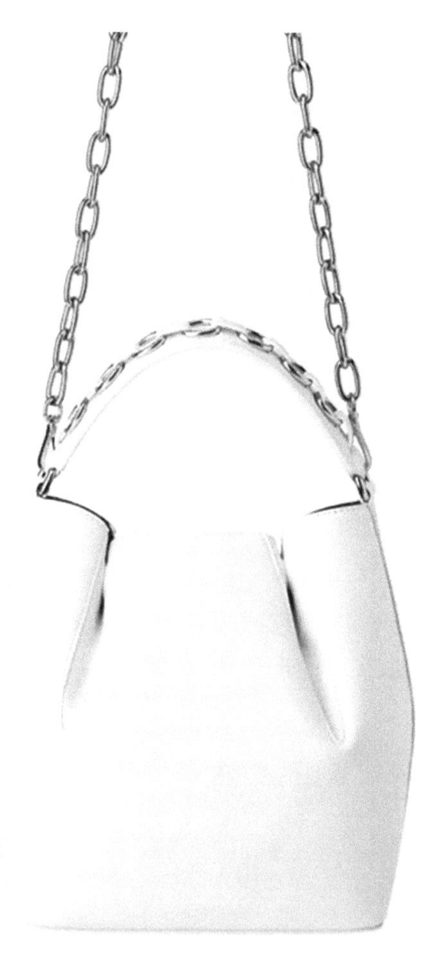

THE MADE TO LOVE COLLECTION

POSITIVE TOOLS TO BUILD HEALTHY RELATIONSHIPS FROM A YOUNG AGE

Made To Love Book

Follow the story of Payton, and her friends as they learn important lessons about behavior, kindness, and respect through fun adventures

Made To Love Jigsaw Puzzle

- 48+ piece puzzles featuring scenes from the Made To Love books

- Engages visual and fine motor skills while reinforcing key lessons

Written & Designed by Vikki Jones

PERSONAL GROWTH & SUCCESS
UNLOCKING YOUR GREATEST POTENTIAL

Life is a journey of constant growth and self-discovery. Often, we find ourselves in a state of complacency, unaware that there is a greater place waiting for us. It is during these uncomfortable moments that we have the opportunity to develop our character, enhance our skills, and prepare ourselves for the next level. Embracing discomfort becomes the key to unlocking our greatest potential. In this editorial, we will explore the importance of pushing through, focusing, and challenging ourselves to reach new heights in life.

1. The Comfort Zone Illusion:

The comfort zone is a deceptive place, where we may feel safe and secure, but it hinders our personal growth. It is in the discomfort that we truly learn and evolve as individuals. Stepping out of our comfort zone allows us to expand our horizons, face new challenges, and discover hidden talents. Embracing discomfort is the first step towards breaking free from the limitations we set for ourselves.

2. Character Development:

When faced with discomfort, we are forced to confront our fears and insecurities. This process builds resilience, determination, and character. Overcoming obstacles strengthens our mental and emotional muscles, enabling us to handle future challenges with greater ease. Embracing discomfort becomes an opportunity for personal growth and self-improvement, shaping us into stronger and more capable individuals.

3. Skill Enhancement:

In the pursuit of our greatest place, we must continuously refine and develop our skills. Embracing discomfort pushes us to acquire new knowledge, learn from our mistakes, and adapt to unfamiliar situations. It is through these experiences that we acquire the expertise and abilities necessary to excel in our chosen fields. Each moment of discomfort becomes an opportunity to sharpen our skills and become better versions of ourselves.

4. Preparation for the Next Level:

Life is a series of stepping stones, and each discomfort we encounter prepares us for the next level. By embracing discomfort, we become better equipped to handle the challenges that lie ahead. Our ability to adapt, persevere, and thrive in uncomfortable situations becomes a valuable asset as we progress towards our goals.

Embracing discomfort is not only about reaching our greatest place but also about preparing ourselves for the journey that follows.

5. Determination and Intentionality:

To embrace discomfort, we must approach it with determination and intentionality. It is not enough to simply endure discomfort; we must actively seek out opportunities for growth and self-improvement. This requires setting clear goals, breaking them down into manageable steps, and committing ourselves to the process.

With a focused mindset and unwavering determination, we can navigate through discomfort and emerge stronger on the other side.

Embracing discomfort is a necessary step in our journey towards self-actualization. It is through these uncomfortable moments that we learn, grow, and prepare ourselves for our greatest place in life. By stepping out of our comfort zone, we develop our character, enhance our skills, and become better equipped to face the challenges that lie ahead. Let us embrace discomfort with determination and intentionality, knowing that our greatest potential awaits us on the other side.

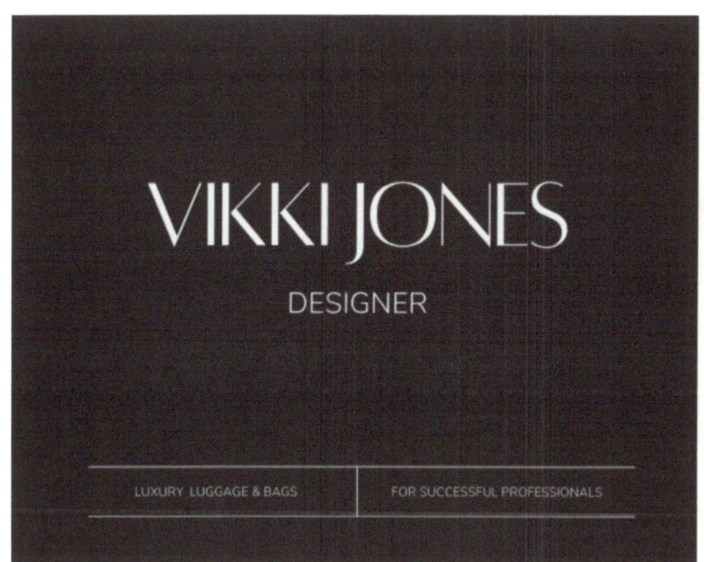

COMFORTABLE CARRYING OPTIONS

Say goodbye to uncomfortable bags. Vikki Jones' designs prioritize comfort, with padded straps, ergonomic handles, and lightweight construction, ensuring a comfortable carrying experience even during long journeys.

Need extra space? Jones' bags feature expandable compartments, allowing you to increase the capacity when needed. Travel with confidence, knowing you have room for souvenirs or extra work documents.

THE HARVEY'S

NEW SPOT ALERT ATL DISCOVER THE SPECTRUM OF CULINARY & BUSINESS EXPERIENCES

Simone and Tim Harvey (Photo Credit: Vikki Jones)

Tim Harvey Prepping for New Spot Alert ATL Showcase

In a city as diverse as Atlanta, the ability to shift between casual and fine dining experiences, from hole-in-the-wall gems to Michelin-star establishments, is a testament to the thriving culinary scene. New Spot Alert ATL, led by Tim and Simone Harvey, embraces the concept of inclusion, empowering individuals to enhance their atmosphere, expand their palate, and indulge in a variety of gastronomic delights. However, their mission extends far beyond the realm of dining, as they also showcase diverse consumer services, such as beauty and grooming, and celebrate small businesses.

Tim Harvey reflects on the humble origins of New Spot Alert ATL, saying, "We started out by simply going out to eat and visiting various places for entertainment and services. We realized that if a place was truly exceptional, why not share it with others? Atlanta attracts people from all walks of life, so we decided to create a platform where we could provide recommendations to a wider audience. It has been an incredibly enjoyable journey for us."

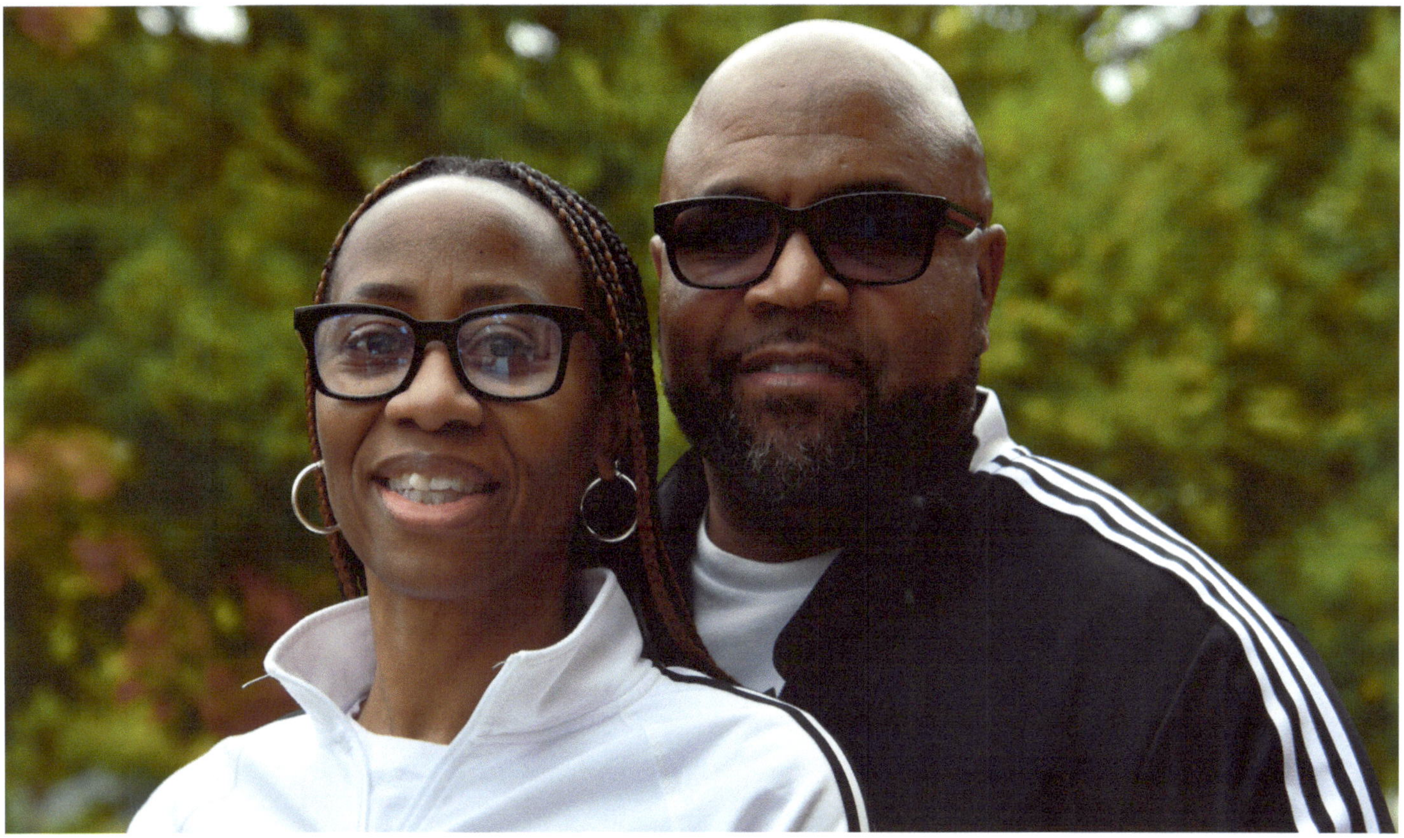

Simone Harvey echoes her husband's sentiment, emphasizing the inclusive nature of their platform, "Just as my husband mentioned, it all started with us going out to eat and posting about it on Facebook, tagging ourselves. Soon enough, we received countless calls from people asking for recommendations when they were visiting Atlanta. That's when we decided to create a dedicated platform for everyone to follow, so they can stay updated with our daily recommendations. When you're coming to the Atlanta Metro area, or any area we visit, just head to our Instagram page, 'New Spot Alert ATL.' There, you'll find a diverse range of recommended restaurants to choose from. And what excites me the most is the quality of services that come with these recommendations."

The beauty of New Spot Alert ATL lies not only in its culinary expertise but also in its celebration of the broader business community.

Tim and Simone Harvey understand the significance of showcasing small businesses, recognizing the unique offerings they bring to the table. By highlighting beauty, grooming, and other consumer services, they not only diversify Atlanta's social landscape but also support the entrepreneurs behind these ventures.

Through New Spot Alert ATL, individuals and tourists can enrich their experiences by venturing outside their comfort zones. The platform acts as a guiding light, illuminating a path that leads to unforgettable memories and remarkable discoveries. Whether it's a cozy neighborhood café, a high-end dining establishment, or a hidden gem tucked away in the city, Tim and Simone Harvey's recommendations promise exceptional service and unforgettable experiences.

So, as you plan your next outing or visit to Atlanta, remember to follow @newspotalertatl on Instagram, TikTok, and other social media platforms.

Discover Atlanta's Hidden Gems!

LOOKING FOR THE HOTTEST NEW SPOTS IN ATLANTA? LOOK NO FURTHER THAN **NEW SPOT ALERT ATL**!

WE PERSONALLY VISIT AND VET EACH LOCATION TO BRING YOU THE BEST OF:

Dining: From upscale to casual eateries, we've got you covered!

Entertainment: Explore exciting venues for a night out on the town!

Beauty: Find businesses to enhance your beauty and self-care routines!

Join our Instagram community @newspotalertatl and let us guide you through Atlanta's culinary and entertainment scene. Trust our recommendations - we've got the inside scoop!

Don't miss out on the newest and best spots in Atlanta!

TikTok: @newspotalertatl

Instagram:@newspotalertatl

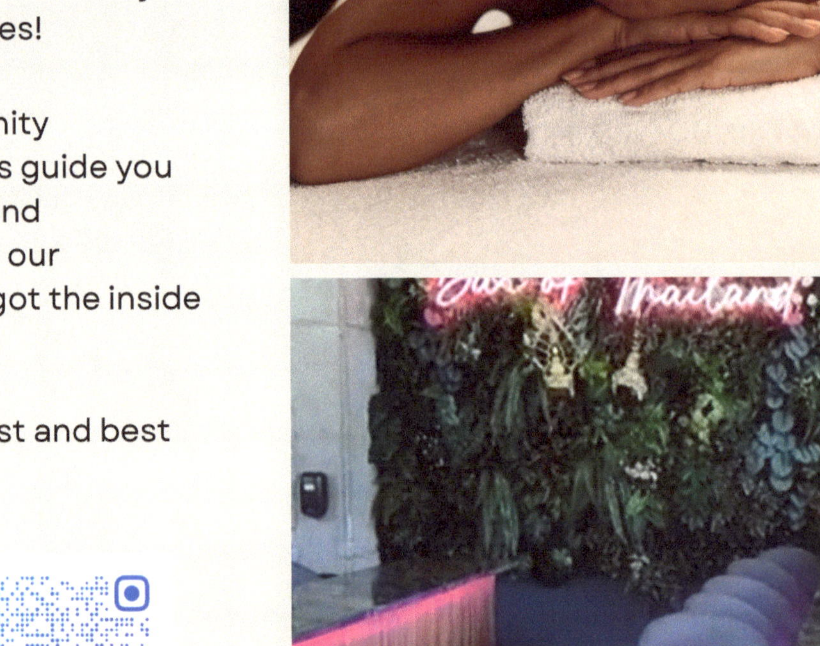

UNLOCK YOUR POWER WITHIN

FACETS OF THE HEART TRANSFORMATION FROM THE INSIDE OUT

- Tap into your inner strength and courage to embrace positive change.
- Dontisha James shares her insights gained from captivating speaking engagements.
- Gain profound knowledge and practical tools to unlock your full potential.
- Embrace the powerful role of faith and spirituality in achieving true transformation.
- Understand the impact of personal transformation on society as a whole.

PURCHASE NOW

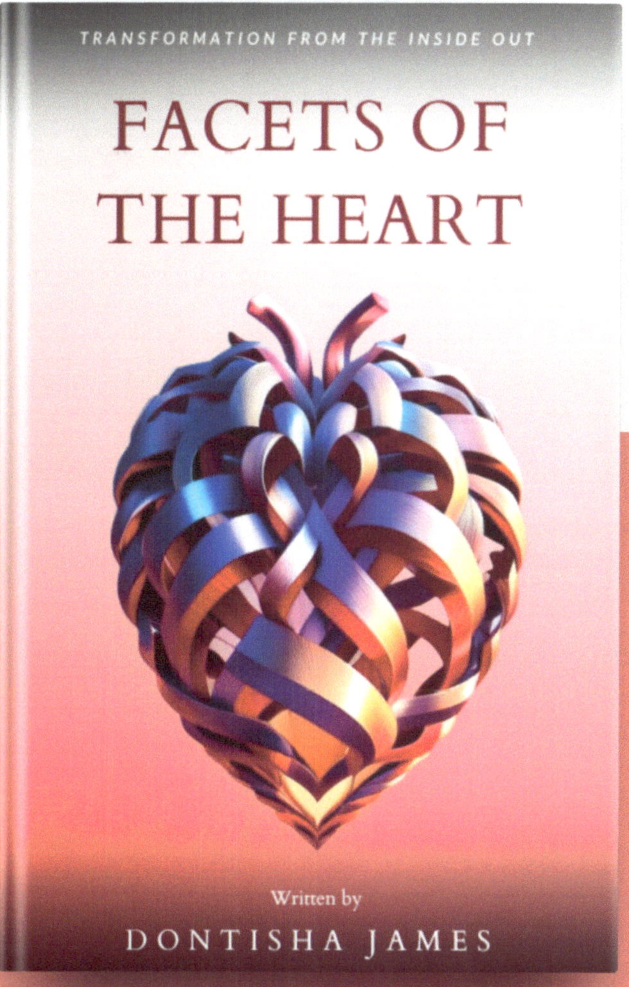

Written by Vikki Jones

BOOSTING SMALL AND MEDIUM-SIZED BUSINESSES:

HOW AI AND CHATGPT CAN HELP

Have you ever wondered how big companies always seem to have the upper hand when it comes to new technologies like Artificial Intelligence (AI)? It's because they have the money and staff to quickly jump on the AI bandwagon and make the most of it, while small and medium-sized businesses (SMEs) struggle to keep up. But shouldn't there be a way for smaller companies to increase their profits and tap into the full potential of AI too?

Well, the good news is that there is hope for SMEs to level the playing field and benefit from AI and the recently released ChatGPT. These fancy tech tools have a lot to offer, but it's understandable that smaller businesses might be hesitant to trust and adopt them. After all, they don't have an army of tech experts at their disposal like the big guys do.

But fear not, because there are practical ways for SMEs to embrace AI and ChatGPT without breaking the bank or feeling overwhelmed. The first step is education and awareness. SMEs need to take the time to learn about the benefits and possibilities that AI and ChatGPT can bring to their operations.

By understanding how these technologies can improve efficiency and productivity in specific areas, SMEs can start reaping the rewards.

Building trust is another crucial factor. AI might seem like a scary and unpredictable thing, but SMEs can ease their worries by partnering with reliable AI providers and starting with small-scale pilot projects. Seeing tangible results and success stories within their own industry will help SMEs gain confidence in AI as a valuable tool for their business.

Collaboration is key too. SMEs can team up with other small businesses or even larger companies to share resources, expertise, and navigate the AI landscape together. By working together, they can overcome the lack of technical talent and benefit from collective knowledge, which will ultimately level the playing field against their bigger competitors.

It's also important for governments and industry associations to lend a helping hand. They can offer incentives, grants, and specialized programs to support SMEs in implementing AI technologies. By creating an environment that promotes knowledge-sharing, collaboration, and innovation, policymakers can empower SMEs to fully embrace AI and unlock its potential.

Yes, the challenges of adopting AI and ChatGPT might seem challenging for SMEs, but it's important to remember that every new technology brings opportunities for growth and success. By seeking knowledge, building trust, embracing collaboration, and taking advantage of supportive policies, small and medium-sized businesses can harness the power of AI and ChatGPT to increase their profits, work more efficiently, and thrive in a competitive market.

PRACTICAL WAYS
SME'S CAN UTILIZE AI

Small and medium-sized enterprises (SMEs) can leverage the power of Artificial Intelligence (AI) in various ways to enhance their operations, improve efficiency, and drive growth.

1. **Customer Service and Support:** AI-powered chatbots and virtual assistants can handle customer inquiries, provide real-time support, and offer personalized recommendations. These AI-driven solutions can streamline customer interactions, reduce response times, and improve customer satisfaction, even outside regular business hours.

2. **Data Analysis and Insights:** AI algorithms can process large volumes of data quickly and accurately, enabling SMEs to gain valuable insights. By analyzing customer behavior, market trends, and operational data, SMEs can make informed decisions, identify patterns, and predict future trends. This helps in optimizing marketing strategies, inventory management, and overall business operations.

3. **Predictive Maintenance:** AI can help SMEs implement predictive maintenance strategies by analyzing data from sensors and machines. By detecting patterns and anomalies, AI algorithms can predict equipment failures or maintenance needs, allowing SMEs to proactively address issues before they escalate. This minimizes downtime, reduces maintenance costs, and extends the lifespan of machinery and assets.

4. **Process Automation:** AI-powered automation can streamline repetitive and time-consuming tasks, freeing up employees to focus on more strategic and value-added activities. SMEs can use AI to automate data entry, invoice processing, inventory management, and other routine tasks, improving operational efficiency and reducing errors.

5. **Sales and Marketing Optimization:** AI can enhance SMEs' sales and marketing efforts by analyzing customer data, identifying leads, and personalizing marketing campaigns. AI algorithms can segment customers based on their preferences, purchase history, and behavior, enabling SMEs to deliver targeted and relevant marketing messages. This helps in boosting conversion rates, increasing customer engagement, and optimizing sales funnels.

6. **Personalized Customer Experiences:** AI enables SMEs to deliver personalized experiences by analyzing customer preferences, behavior, and past interactions. AI algorithms can recommend products, content, and services tailored to each customer's specific needs and interests. This enhances customer satisfaction, loyalty, and drives repeat business.

7. **Market Research and Competitive Analysis:** SMEs can leverage AI to gather and analyze market data, customer reviews, social media sentiment, and competitor information. AI-powered tools can provide valuable insights into market trends, consumer preferences, and competitive intelligence. This helps SMEs make data-driven decisions, identify market gaps, and develop competitive strategies.

8. **Virtual Collaboration and Communication:** With the rise of remote work, AI-powered virtual collaboration tools can facilitate communication, project management, and knowledge sharing among remote teams. AI-driven solutions can automate scheduling, generate meeting summaries, and provide real-time language translation, enabling SMEs to collaborate effectively across borders and time zones.

Stacey McWhorton,
the Owner of
Sweet Stacey's Bakery

Photo Credit: Vikki Jones.

SWEET STACEY'S: A REMARKABLE JOURNEY OF DETERMINATION AND DELICIOUS CREATIONS

Written by Vikki Jones

Inspiration can be found in the simplest of places, and sometimes it takes just one person's unwavering belief in themselves to ignite a flame of courage within us all. Stacey McWhorton, the owner of Sweet Stacey's bakery, is one such person who exemplifies the power of self-belief and determination. Her journey from a simple dream to a thriving bakery is nothing short of remarkable.

When asked about the secret to her success, Stacey shared a powerful mantra that has guided her every step of the way: "Bet on yourself. Always believe in yourself. Even when no one else believes in you, you believe in yourself." These words are a testament to her resilience and unwavering spirit, even in the face of doubt and adversity.

Stacey's path to entrepreneurship was marked by bold moves and resourcefulness. She made the courageous decision to sell her house to fund her bakery venture, putting everything on the line to pursue her passion. It was during the planning of her own wedding that she discovered her love for cake decorating, setting in motion the realization that she could turn her baking skills into a flourishing business.

But Stacey's journey was not without its challenges. She faced financial hurdles, particularly during the unexpected trials brought on by the pandemic. However, her determination and resourcefulness shone through. With her son by her side, Stacey found ingenious ways to make things work. From tiling the floor to painting the walls, she meticulously crafted a welcoming space for her bakery, taking full advantage of the opportunities that came her way.

The fruits of Stacey's labor are evident in the mouthwatering treats that adorn the shelves of Sweet

Stacey's Bakery. Her desserts are baked fresh daily, offering a delectable array of flavors to satisfy any sweet tooth. Customers not only have the pleasure of visiting the charming storefront, but they can also conveniently place orders online, including customized cakes and desserts for special events.

Stacey's entrepreneurial journey goes beyond her delicious creations. She shares valuable insights on starting a business, overcoming obstacles, and taking savvy measures to ensure success. Her story is a reminder that dreams can be pursued with passion and dedication, regardless of the challenges that may arise along the way.

To experience the magic of Stacey's unwavering determination and to indulge in her tantalizing creations, a visit to Sweet Stacey's Bakery is a must. Whether in-person at their inviting storefront or through online orders, the taste sensations will leave you craving more. Connect with Stacey's journey and explore her delectable world at www.sweetstaceys.com.

Stacey McWhorton's culinary expertise combined with her incredible story of perseverance will undoubtedly leave you inspired and ready to chase your own dreams. So take a leap of faith, bet on yourself, and let Stacey's journey be a guiding light on your own path to success.

NEED MARKETING?

CONTACT US!

VMHMAGAZINE.COM

EXPERIENCE THE
EPITOME OF LUXURY AND
UNMATCHED ELEGANCE
WITH A'LASHELL
LIPSTICKS
A'LASHELL
WWW.ALASHELL.COM

The Home Depot Foundation Invests $6 Million in Skilled Trades Training - New Scholarship and Entrepreneurship Partnerships

The Home Depot Foundation announced an incremental investment of more than $6 millionin skilled trades training and launched new strategic partnerships to address the nearly 400,000 job openings across the construction industry. With these philanthropic grants, the *Foundation's Path to Pro program* launched a brand new entrepreneurship program and will provide free, skilled trades training and scholarships for more veterans, military families, high school students and separating service members.

To serve aspiring entrepreneurs within the skilled trades industry, The Home Depot Foundation is partnering with Bunker Labs to introduce an entrepreneurship program designed to guide U.S. military veterans and military spouses through the process of establishing a successful business foundation. During the 8-week program, participants will gain industry-specific mentorship, learn about market segmentation, how to address specific customer profiles and design a business plan for launch. The program's virtual offering makes it accessible to participants nationwide.

The Foundation is also expanding its Path to Pro scholarship program with grants to SkillPointe Foundation, its partner since 2021, and through a new partnership with Folds of Honor. Military scholarships through Folds of Honor extend financial support to qualifying veterans and military family members entering or enrolled in accredited skilled trade schools.

"We're expanding our current training programs and creating new avenues to steadily fill the country's skilled labor gap with in-demand talent," said The Home Depot Foundation's executive director, Shannon Gerber. "Diversifying our approach with additional entrepreneurship and scholarship programs helps ensure we're reaching more communities with free training opportunities and creating sustainable change for the industry."

The Home Depot Foundation extended its grant to long-time partner Home Builders Institute to broaden its Path to Pro high school and military programs. The two organizations will continue to provide no-cost PACT curriculum certification for more than 1,200 separating military members annually, 11th and 12th grade students and Title 1 schools nationwide.

The Home Depot Foundation's skilled trades training program, Path to Pro, launched in 2018 with a $50 million commitment to train the next generation of skilled tradespeople, diversify the trades industry, and address the growing labor shortage in the U.S. The Foundation's trades-focused partnerships have introduced more than 200,000 people to the skilled trades and have trained more than 41,000 participants through programming available to youth, high school students, underserved communities and separating U.S. military.

Beyond the Foundation's work in this area, The Home Depot's Path to Pro Network connects skilled tradespeople to professional contractors and job openings. *For more information and to find skilled trades resources available in English and Spanish, visit PathtoPro.com.*

THE BOOKSHELF

VMH PUBLISHING

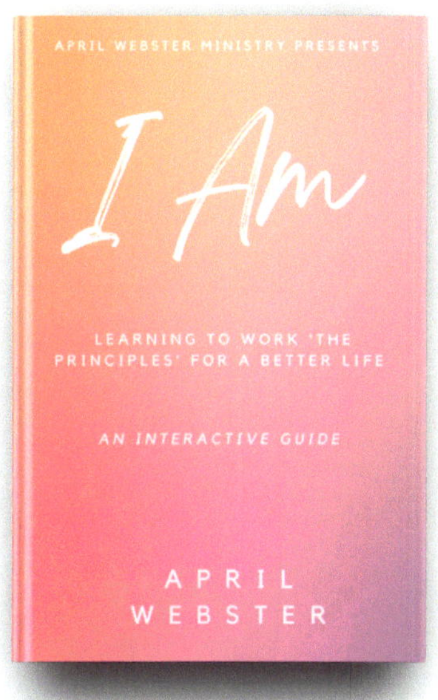

I AM - Learning To Work 'The Principles' For a Better Life

In this book, Dr. April Webster explores twelve affirmations to declare inward strength to her readers. I AM is a metaphysical name of the spiritual self. It is the presence of God with in you. When the words I AM are spoken it is a declaration. I AM is the mere fact of our existence and once you become aware of it you hold the power in your words. Dr. Webster has personally discovered the power of spoken words. This is not a book to be read only once then put away on a book shelf or in a storage bin. This book is intended to be read and repeated over and over until one becomes fully aware of who they really are called to be. This book requires the readers to take action.

By following these principles, you hold the power of transforming your life to another level beyond your current position. Dr. Webster provides the steps needed to act and apply these principles to your life. You will walk and operate in another dimension once you become aware of who you really are.

Bootstrap
Start Where You Are with What You Have

Have a great business idea but no capital? It's possible to build and grow a profitable business without external help or capital. With today's digital technology, a business can be established with little money and succeed. Within this book you will find the framework to start, build and scale a business successfully without tapping into another's bank account. "Bootstrap" serves as an empowering and encouraging tool for aspiring entrepreneurs who may feel discouraged by their lack of resources or access to capital. By demonstrating that success can be achieved through resourcefulness and determination, the book motivates individuals to think creatively, tap into their skills and strengths, and embark on their entrepreneurial journey.

My Best Kept Secret Memoir

"My Best Kept Secret Memoir" is a powerful and inspiring collection of personal stories shared by the author, aimed at empowering women who have endured incidents of abuse. Through her heartfelt narratives, she aims to encourage healing, resilience, and the strength to break free from the shackles of abuse. This memoir is an essential read for anyone seeking to reclaim their lives.

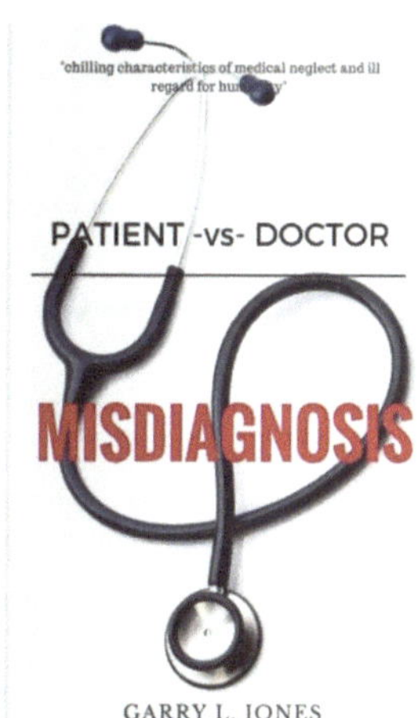

Misdiagnosis: Prostate Cancer Survivor

In his book, Fmr. Lt. Garry L. Jones teaches patients how to prevent delayed or misdiagnosis. After suffering years of recurring infections Jones eventually learned the root cause of his suffering - prostate cancer.

JASMINE TOOKES JOINS ANNE KLEIN TO COMMEMORATE THE BATTLE OF VERSAILLES ANNIVERSARY

Written by Vikki Jones | Photos Courtesy: Atelier PR

In a powerful collaboration that celebrates both fashion history and female empowerment, supermodel and entrepreneur Jasmine Tookes has joined forces with iconic American brand Anne Klein. Together, they are set to commemorate the 50th anniversary of the historic Battle of Versailles, a turning point for American sportswear in the global fashion scene.

Anne Klein, a brand synonymous with timeless style, is marking this significant year with the release of their Fall/Winter 2023 fashion campaign. Featuring Jasmine Tookes as the face of the campaign, the collection captures the essence of a modern woman navigating a fast-paced world with grace and confidence. With this partnership, Anne Klein and Jasmine Tookes pay homage to the brand's legacy and the everlasting impact of the Battle of Versailles.

Photographed on the bustling streets of New York City by the renowned Tom Schirmacher, the Anne Klein Fall/Winter '23 campaign brings to life a collection of rich classics, perfectly suited for any occasion. Jasmine Tookes effortlessly showcases these designs, adding her own touch of elegance and personality to each look.

The Battle of Versailles, an event that revolutionized global fashion and propelled American sportswear to the forefront, holds deep significance for Anne Klein. To honor this pivotal moment, Anne Klein will collaborate with NYFW: The Talks to host a panel discussion titled "Battle of Versailles 50: The Making of Fashion History." Moderated by Jasmine Tookes herself, the panel will feature esteemed guests including designer Stephen Burrows, the last surviving designer from

the original ten, Donna Karan, Anne Klein's right hand during that time, and trailblazing models Alva Chinn and Pat Cleveland, whose unforgettable catwalk styles forever changed the industry. Jameel Spencer, CMO in Residence for Anne Klein, speaks proudly about the brand's legacy, stating, "We take immense pride in honoring Anne's legacy and keeping that flame alive. The Battle of Versailles not only showcased Anne Klein's work on a global stage, but it also sparked social change, racial awareness, and American magic. As we celebrate multiple milestones this year, including what would have been our founder's 100th birthday, we are thrilled to partner with Jasmine Tookes to recognize the strength of diverse women impacting the world positively, all while exuding style and grace."

Jasmine Tookes, shared her enthusiasm for the collaboration, saying, "*I am thrilled to be a small part of this storied brand founded by a powerful woman. My power as a woman lies in my positivity and being able to serve as a role model for mothers and businesswomen, gracefully managing it all with style.*"

This collaboration between Jasmine Tookes and Anne Klein not only pays tribute to the past but also paves the way for a future where diverse women continue to inspire and empower individuals worldwide. Together, they showcase the timeless appeal of wardrobe choices that transcend trends and exude a sense of confidence and individuality. *For more information on Jasmine, visit www.thelionsmanagement.com, or @TheLionsMgmt on Instagram.*

5 Tips to Manage Money Smarter

There's more to managing your money than paying your bills and successfully avoiding overdraft charges (although those are definitely steps in the right direction). Effectively managing your money takes time and planning, but the payoff may be a stronger financial future.

Create a budget. Some people avoid making a monthly budget because they think they don't need one. However, having a clear idea of the money coming in and going out of your bank account each month can help you make better spending decisions. A budget doesn't have to be complicated; it can be as simple as a spreadsheet that lists your monthly income and expenses. Be sure to consider long-term debt, like student loans, and treat your savings account as a payee you owe each month.

Track your spending. In a similar vein, it's a good idea to see where your non-bill-related spending goes. For example, you may stop by the grocery store more frequently than you realize, and each of those trips is likely going to cost you more than if you limited it to just once or twice a week. Many banks and credit institutions offer charts and graphs that break down your spending so you can see exactly where your money is going and use that information to make adjustments.

Research big purchases. What constitutes "big" may vary depending on your circumstances and financial status, but regardless of the dollar amount, doing some due diligence before purchases is a good idea. The average millennial will do 4.6 hours of research before buying a big-ticket item like a mattress or car, according to a survey conducted by OnePoll on behalf of Mattress Firm.

Millennials are also likely to seek input from others, with one in five consulting four or more people for their opinions on a purchase.

"Doing research before making a big purchase can make all the difference," said Timothy Mayes, Mattress Firm's senior manager of eCommerce merchandising. "There are several resources available such as online reviews, blogs and even guides on the best time to buy that can help save you money on larger purchases. If you find yourself overwhelmed with too many options, recommendations from friends and family are the best resources to help you narrow down your choices."

Prepare for emergencies. If a single unexpected event would cripple you financially, it's a good idea to build an emergency fund that could help you weather through a storm. A job loss, accident or illness would substantially alter your income, expenses or both, so having at least a few months of salary stashed in savings could make a major difference in how long that unfortunate scenario affects your life.

Finance purchases responsibly. Building credit takes time and responsibility, but if you don't ever borrow money, you won't have a chance to earn the rates reserved for exceptional credit holders. Financing a moderately sized purchase, such as a mattress, is a good starting point. It may be out of reach for a cash payment, but the balance you carry could be paid in a reasonably short timeframe. To build good credit, always make payments on time and make monthly payments larger than the minimum payment – which is usually just the interest – so you're actually paying down the principal. Following these tips and taking advantage of product sites that offer resources and information on a potential purchase may aid in your long-term financial health. Find more information at MattressFirm.com/blog.

www.ingramcontent.com/pod-product-compliance
Lightning Source LLC
Chambersburg PA
CBHW042126150726
48005CB00029B/653